Extra

Add **un** or **dis** to finish these words.

1 ____kind   2 ____agree   3 ____happy

4 ____tidy   5 ____true   6 ____used

7 ____do   8 ____like   9 ____appear

10 ____trust   11 ____sure   12 ____tie

13 ____cover   14 ____obey   15 ____load

Extension

A Find the eight **un** and **dis** words in the wordsearch.

B Write the words you have found.

b	u	n	t	r	u	e	o	b
l	n	d	d	u	n	d	o	m
g	t	i	i	l	h	i	p	u
n	i	s	s	r	v	s	f	n
s	d	o	l	m	t	a	c	c
k	y	b	i	v	k	g	j	o
n	e	e	k	r	h	r	g	v
q	w	y	e	h	b	e	n	e
d	i	s	a	p	p	e	a	r

3

UNIT 16

soft c

race

Focus

Write the words next to the things you can see in the picture.

cereal   face   ice   mice   police   price   race   slice

Key Words

ice
rice
price

mice
dice
nice

ace
race
face

city
centre
cell
cellar
cereal

4

Extra

Write the word that matches the picture.

1 cereal or cellar

2 face or race

3 dice or mice

4 lace or race

5 city or circle

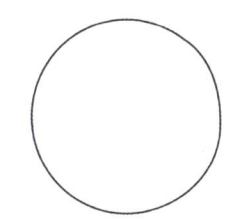

6 juicy or spicy

7 fence or pence

8 chance or dance

9 notice or police

Extension

Write a sentence using each of these **soft c** words.

1 police _____

2 fence _____

3 race _____

4 mice _____

5

UNIT 17

soft g ge dge

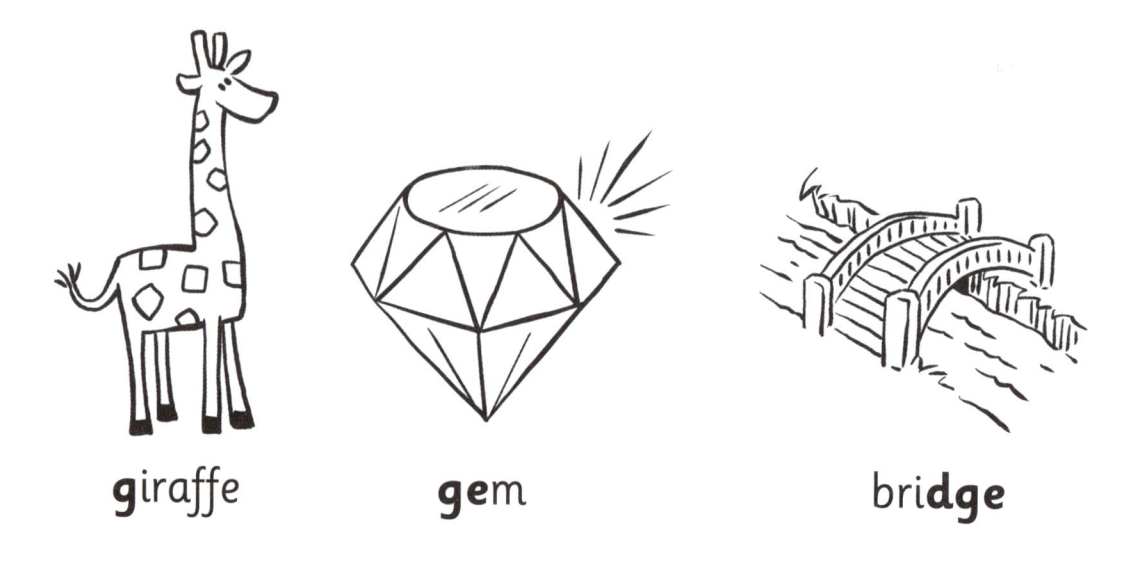

giraffe   gem   bridge

Focus

Write the words next to the things you can see in the picture.

| badge | bridge | cabbage | cage |
| giraffe | hedge | orange | page |

Key Words

gem
gentle
giraffe

age
urgent

large
huge
tragic
village

bridge
badge
hedge
judge

6

Extra

Choose a word from the box to finish the sentences.

| bridge | gentle | giraffe | hedge | large | village |

1 A dog jumped off a _____ into the water!

2 I want a _____ slice of cake.

3 I watched a baby _____ with its mother.

4 Ellie hid behind the _____.

5 The child was _____ when she stroked the cat.

6 My grandmother lives in a _____.

Extension

Colour the letters that make the words.
Copy the new words.

1 | t | b | f | a | h | d | r | w | g | e | b_____

2 | a | h | g | n | e | r | s | m | k | l | g_____

3 | t | o | l | a | e | w | r | g | b | e | l_____

4 | d | s | h | f | e | d | i | g | v | e | h_____

7

UNIT 18

le el al il endings

cand**le**

cam**el**

pet**al**

foss**il**

Key Words

candle
handle
paddle
middle
angle
bangle
rectangle
camel
chisel
jewel
satchel
pedal
petal
signal
usual
fossil
tonsil

Focus

Write the words next to the things you can see in the picture.

| camel | candle | fossil | jewel |
| pedal | petal | rectangle | saddle |

jewel

8

Extra

Add **le**, **el**, **al** and **il** to finish these words.

1 cam_____   2 sign_____   3 foss_____
4 cand_____   5 hand_____   6 jew_____
7 ped_____   8 pet_____   9 tons_____
10 lab_____   11 med_____   12 jung_____
13 mod_____   14 hospit_____ 15 rectang_____

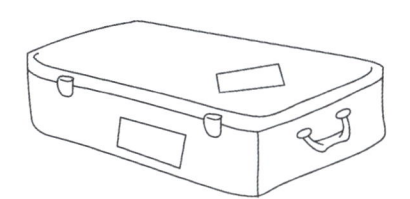

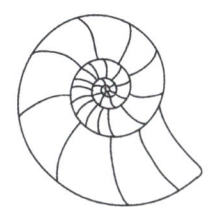

Extension

Choose the best word for each gap.

1 | handle   candle |

The _____ holder has a _____.

2 | paddle   middle |

I dropped the _____ in the _____ of the river.

3 | jewel   camel |

The _____ carried the _____ across the desert.

4 | fossil   chisel |

A _____ was used to free the _____.

5 | pedal   usual |

My bike _____ fell off, as _____!

9

UNIT 19

adding 's or s

girl**s** box**es** bab**ies**

Focus

Write the words next to the things you can see in the picture.

girls   buses   mum's cats
nan's bushes   dad's boxes

nan's bushes

Key Words

mum's
nan's
postman's
dad's
sister's
brother's

cats
girls
roads

buses
bushes
boxes

10

Extra

Write a sentence using each of these phrases. Add the missing apostrophes.

1 my brothers bike   _____
2 the schools ball   _____
3 a teachers key   _____
4 the cows calf   _____

Extension

Remember:

If a noun ends with **s**, **x**, **ch** or **sh**, we add **es** to make it plural.

   bus   +   **es** = bus**es**

To make a noun plural that ends with a **y**, change the **y** to **i** before adding **es**.

   story   stor**ies**

But if the letter **before** the y is a **vowel** (a e i o u) – **just add s**.

   day   day**s**

Write the correct spelling of the plural word to match each picture.

1 girls or girles

2 boxs or boxes

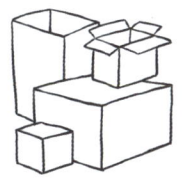

3 brushs or brushes

4 toys or toies

5 carrots or carrotes

6 babys or babies

UNIT 20

y ey endings

baby monkey

Focus

Write the words next to the things you can see in the picture.

baby	chimney	cry	donkey
fly	happy	key	monkey

Key Words

cry
fly
dry
try
spy
reply
July

key
donkey
monkey
chimney
valley

baby
copy
happy
merry
sorry

chimney

12

Extra

Add **y** or **ey** to finish these words.

1 cr_____ 2 vall_____ 3 k_____

4 Jul_____ 5 donk_____ 6 sorr_____

7 tr_____ 8 chimn_____ 9 bab_____

10 repl_____ 11 happ_____ 12 monk_____

13 dr_____ 14 merr_____ 15 sp_____

Extension

> Remember what happens when we need to add 's' to the end of words ending in **y**:
>
> If the letter **before** the y is a **vowel** (a e i o u) – **just add s**.
>
> key + s = keys
>
> If the letter **before** the y is **any other letter** – **change the y to i and add es**.
>
> fly + s = flies

Write the plural word.

1  monkey _____

2 spy _____

3  baby _____

4  valley _____

5  trolley _____

6  butterfly _____

13

UNIT 21

adding
ing ed er

running   runner

Focus

Write the words next to the things you can see in the picture.

| dropped | jumped | jumping | wagging |

jumped

Key Words

wag
wagging
wagged

beg
begging
begged

sit
sitting
sitter

run
running
runner

patting
dropping

Extra

Look at what happens when we need to add endings to very short words:

If the letter **before** the last letter is a **vowel** (a e i o u) – **double the last letter**.

  hop + ing = ho**pp**ing

If the letter **before** the last letter is **any other letter** – <u>don't</u> **double the last letter**.

  ju**m**p + ing = jumping

Do these word sums.

1 drop   + ing   = _____
2 cry   + ing   = _____
3 wet   + ing   = _____
4 skip   + ing   = _____
5 run   + ing   = _____
6 beg   + ing   = _____
7 smash + ing   = _____
8 call   + ing   = _____
9 copy   + ing   = _____
10 kick   + ing   = _____

Extension

Remember, if we want to add **ing** to a 'magic' e word, first we need to take off the e, like this:

  bake + **ing** = baking

To add **ed** or **er** to a 'magic' e word, we also need to take off the e, like this:

  bake + **ed** = baked   bake + **er** = baker

Do these word sums.

1 race   + ing = _____
2 shade + ed   = _____
3 glide + er   = _____
4 pace   + er   = _____
5 glue   + ed   = _____
6 rope   + ing = _____
7 vote   + ed   = _____
8 tune   + ing = _____
9 arrive + ing = _____
10 wipe   + er   = _____

UNIT 22

silent letters

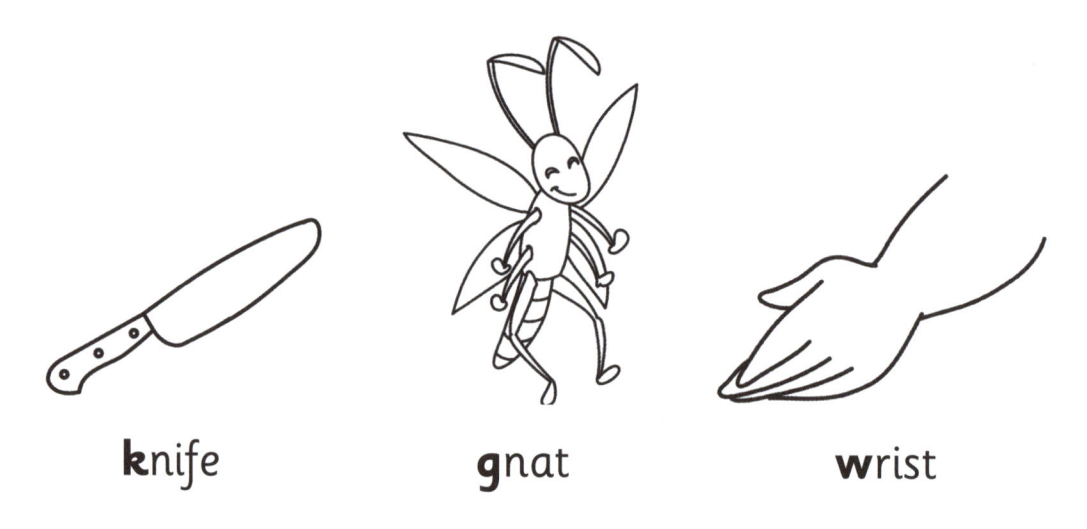

knife **g**nat **w**rist

Focus

Write the words next to the things you can see in the picture.

| gnaw | wrong | knee | knife |
| knock | knot | wrist | write |

Key Words

knee
kneel
knew
knife
knit
knot
knock

gnat
gnaw

wrap
write
wrist
wrestle
wrong

knock

16

Extra

Circle the silent letter in each of these words.

1 w r i t e   2 g n a w   3 k n o t

4 k n i f e   5 w r e c k   6 w r e s t l e

7 k n e e l   8 w r a p   9 g n a t

10 w r i s t   11 w r o n g   12 k n o c k

Extension

A Write three words with the silent letter **k**.

_____   _____   _____

B Write three words with the silent letter **g**.

_____   _____   _____

C Write three words with the silent letter **w**.

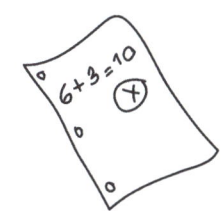

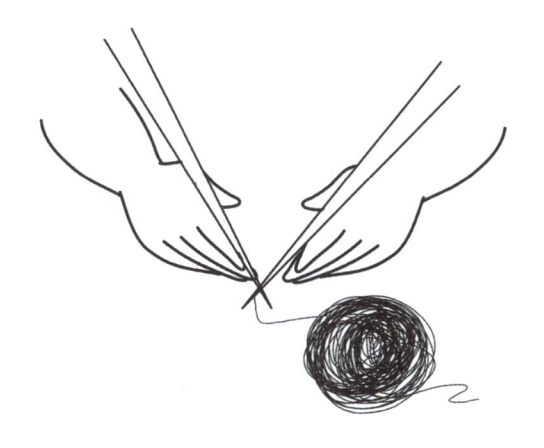

_____   _____   _____

UNIT 23

wa
qua

watch

s**qua**sh

Focus

Write the words next to the things you can see in the picture.

| squabble | squash | swamp | swan |
| wash | wasp | watch | water |

Key Words

was
wasp
wash
want
wand
water
watch

swan
swap

war
warm

quantity
squash

swamp

18

Extra

Choose a word from the box to finish the sentences.
Use each word once.

| quantity | squash | swan | swap | wash | water |

1 I must _____ my hands before tea.

2 Can I _____ my drink for yours?

3 The _____ glided up the river.

4 Alex was very hot so had to drink lots of _____.

5 We had to _____ into a small tent when it rained.

6 We collected a large _____ of litter.

Extension

Colour the letters that make the **wa** word.
Copy the new word.

1 h w l k a t r e y r   w_____

2 a s p w t a b v n i   s_____

3 c u w s a j t c h   w_____

4 k w d a g b s n o p   w_____

UNIT 24

adding less ful ness ment ly

pain**ful**

care**less**

agree**ment**

happi**ness**

quick**ly**

Key Words

wishful
painful
careful

careless
homeless
fearless

agreement
department
enjoyment

happiness
laziness
silliness

slowly
quickly
happily

Focus

Write the words next to the things you can see in the picture.

painful   careless   enjoyment
laziness   wishful

wishful

20

Extra

How many words can you make by joining these words and patterns?

care		ful
colour		less
fear	+	
home		
hope		
pain		
use		
wish		

_____   _____   _____

_____   _____   _____

_____   _____   _____

_____   _____   _____

_____   _____   _____

Extension

Choose four of the words you have made above. Write each of them into a sentence.

1 Word: _____

_____

2 Word: _____

_____

3 Word: _____

_____

4 Word: _____

_____

UNIT 25

shortened words

Key Words

I'm
I'll
I've
I'd

she's
he's
it's
there's

don't
isn't
doesn't
didn't

won't
can't

Focus

Draw a line between the contraction and the two words that make it.

I'm	do not
don't	I have
there's	I am
I've	there is
isn't	he is
he's	I would
I'd	is not
doesn't	does not

22

Extra

Write a sentence using each of these contractions.

isn't _____

he'd _____

don't _____

they've _____

she's _____

Extension

A Write three contractions using the word **is**, like this:

it's _____   _____   _____

B Write three contractions using the word **not**.

_____   _____   _____

C Write three of the contractions you have made in sentences.

_____

_____

_____

UNIT **26**

tion

frac**tion**

Focus

Write the words next to the things you can see in the picture.

direction   fraction   instruction
invention   question   station

Key Words

question
motion
nation
fiction

station
relation
education

action
fraction

election
section
direction

suction
destruction
instruction

HOW TO MAKE FUN FISH PIZZA

direction

24

Extra

Write the correct word to match the picture.

1 motion or question

2 station or relation

3 election or section

4 fraction or action

5 fiction or nation

6 instruction or suction

7 education or station

8 action or attraction

9 infection or section

Extension

Write a sentence using each of these **tion** words.

1 infection

2 relation

3 station

4 instruction

25

UNIT 27

homophones

right   write

Focus

Write the words next to the things you can see in the picture.

flour   flower   rain
rein   right   write

Key Words

be
bee

new
knew

there
their
they're

for
four

hole
whole

right
write

26

Extra

Write the words in the box next to their clues.

| blew | blue | ewe | knew | new | right | write | you |

1. a pen or pencil put on paper   _____

   correct   _____

2. something you already know   _____

   something that hasn't been used   _____

3. something that has moved by air   _____

   a colour   _____

4. a female sheep   _____

   the opposite of "me"   _____

Extension

Choose the best word for each gap.

1. | knew   new |

   I _____ the _____ dress would look lovely.

2. | right   write |

   Jacob was _____, he could also _____ with his left hand.

3. | ewe   you |

   Did _____ see the _____ giving birth to the lamb?

4. | blew   blue |

   The _____ sailing boat _____ close to the rocks.

5. | their   there |

   Look over _____, _____ dog has run into a shop!

27

UNIT **28**

y + er
y + est
y + ed

happy   happier   happiest

Focus

Write the words next to the things you can see in the picture.

happy   messy   muddy   sleepy   cry

Key Words

happy
pretty
smelly
moody
cheeky
sleepy
messy
muddy

copy

cry
reply
try

Extra

Make these words.

> Remember, to add **er**, **est** or **ed** to words that end with **y** we usually change the **y** to **i**.
>
> bossy + er = bossier   chilly + est + chilliest   try + ed = tried

1 cheeky + er   =   cheekier
2 smelly + est =   _____
3 cry   + ed   =   _____
4 dusty   + est =   _____
5 cloudy + er   =   _____
6 reply   + ed   =   _____
7 copy   + ed   =   _____
8 noisy   + er   =   _____

Extension

Add a missing word ending in **er** or **est** to finish the sentences.
Use the words in the box to help.

| lucky | messy | windy | funny | muddy |

1 Today is the _____ day since the storm.

2 My boots are _____ than my brother's.

3 My sister's room is the _____ room in the house!

4 Mr Kaur told a _____ joke than Mr Golding.

5 Li felt she was the _____ girl ever when she got a puppy.

Workbook 2B: Progress check

Can you help the bee find its way back to the hive by colouring the units you've completed?

Unit 15
un dis

Unit 16
soft c

Unit 17
soft
g ge
dge

Unit 18
le el al il
endings

Unit 19
adding
's or s

Unit 20
y ey
endings

Unit 21
adding
ing ed er